The Second Waldorf Song Book

The Second
Waldorf Song Book

Collected and arranged
by Brien Masters

Floris Books

First published in 1993 by Floris Books

Photocopying

British Library CIP Data

The second Waldorf song book.
264.2

ISBN 0-86315-135-3

Typeset by Seton Music Graphics Ltd, Co Cork
Printed in Great Britain
by the Cromwell Press, Wilts.

Contents

Introduction

This collection of part-songs has been made partly as a natural sequence to the *Waldorf Song Book* and partly as a response to popular request. It contains most versions of part-singing that will be required in the classroom and will, hopefully, have much to offer other groups of singers outside school. The variety possible in choral combinations has been one of the guiding factors in making this selection. It includes rounds, melodies with descant, two- and three-part songs for equal and for mixed voices, settings for soprano, alto, tenor and bass and a few pieces for slightly larger choirs.

For good measure, a new genre (new, as far as the author is aware) has been created in which the melody may be sung above by female voices, with tenor and bass providing the "accompaniment", or with the melody sung below by male voices, soprano and alto singing the accompanying parts. Thus there are three parts to be learnt, each of four voices singing two of them; this is quite economical on rehearsal time and can help newly hatched four-part choirs find the strength in their wings more quickly, while the music can take full flight without too much (weary) part learning.

It is not so widely known that Rudolf Steiner's (1861–1925) recommendation for the right age at which to begin part-singing was with ten to eleven-year-olds. This coincides with Class 5 in Steiner (Waldorf) schools and will perhaps gain some clarity from the following comments.

Rounds are started in the previous year age nine to ten. Strictly speaking they are not in the same category as part-singing. Nevertheless, in this volume a few are included because they are excellent for warming up and, although choirs always have their own "favourites", a few new ones are always welcome "in the club". Descants, in which the additional part is like a tune in itself and basically above the melody (as in pre-diatonic music), can be seen in the same pedagogical light, that is, as usable in the year preceding part-singing. In part-singing proper a more "divided" form of consciousness is both implied and fostered.

An amusing personal anecdote was recently told by Barry Tuckwell, one of the world's leading horn-players. His family being musical, it was taken for granted that he too would be. Among the first instruments that he "tried" were those played by his father and mother. With the violin, despite the fact that he had a good example to follow, he felt very ham-fisted when it came to all the dexterous passage-work required of fiddlers. So after a time of struggle a change was made, to the organ. But help! Three staves to read at once, fistfuls of notes and dangling feet — out of sight.— getting into a kind of tangled extension of one's boot-laces, not to mention the baffling array of stops. One wrong one, and instead of a computer bleep, a kind of apocalyptic admonition thunders from the organ loft. Finally the family's last shreds of genetic pride had to be swallowed and it was decided that perhaps the only thing left was the French horn.

What a blissful home-coming this proved to be for him! He related: Only one note to read at a time, only one note to play at a time and only one hole to blow into ...

By a similar token one can see that it is unaccompanied monody — the "solo" song, with its one note at a time and the stream of its musical breath constantly flowing through one soul — that is all that the very young child (up to age nine) needs in singing.

But after this age, a further need arises. It is a need intricately connected with what many educationists have observed and what Rudolf Steiner frequently referred to in his commentary on child development as the stage of the "ninth/tenth year." At this age, a new attitude to life finds its inception — a new mode of looking at the world: what formerly was united, now is in parts. This mode requires careful handling in every respect. In music, in addition to the "song" which expresses all (how anachronistic and superfluous a folk-song setting can sometimes feel), the soul can now be nourished by the part-song. This is using the term generically and not in the pedagogically differentiated way indicated above and incorporated into the structure of this book.

For as soon as there is a second part, unity can be experienced in a new way. The "new mode" soul — and we are mostly on this side of the fence — discovers unity not within the various parts (two, three, four or more) but by singing the parts together:

musically and socially. The rehearsal work that this entails should obviously be experienced as having a particular musical aim. However, this goal may be not all that frequently attained, while the social pleasure in the journey shared can be felt each time. Moreover, while the individual parts are learnt, more and more of the music is opened up, for all to enjoy equally.

To those who get social satisfaction from this process of learning, as much as musical satisfaction from the performing (or merely the singing through) of part-songs, this collection is heartily dedicated.

Brien Masters
Michael Hall
April 1993

Rounds and Canons

1. Dona Nobis Pacem

Do - na, do - na, do - na___ no - bis,

Do - na___, do - na___ no - bis pa - cem, Do - -

- na no - bis pa - - - cem,

Do - na no - bis pa - cem.

2. Michaelmas Song

Con forza ma non pesante ♩. = 80

Wind in the trees blows loud for sum - mer's last song,

Thresh - ing the boughs___, pelt - ing the leaves a - long___.

Sleep - ers___ a - wake, hark___ to the word of the

wind, Break - ing old sum - mer's dull, drow - sy
spell, Show us the way____, go____ with thy spear be -
- fore, Forge____ us the fu - ture ____, thou
Mi - cha - ël, Forge us the fu - ture,
Thou Mi - cha - ël____.

2. Frost on the ground at misty dawning shines bright,
   Cracking the clod, lining the twigs with white.
   Sleepers awake, hark to the word of the frost,
   Breaking old summer's...

3. Myriad stars shine in the frosty clear skies,
   Outshining all, the meteor earthward flies.
   Sleepers awake, hark to the word of the star,
   Breaking old summer's...

4. With hearts aglow men mark the changing fresh world,
   When from the stars Michaël's spear is hurled.
   Sleepers awake, hark to the word of the world,
   Breaking old summer's...

13

3. Sanctus

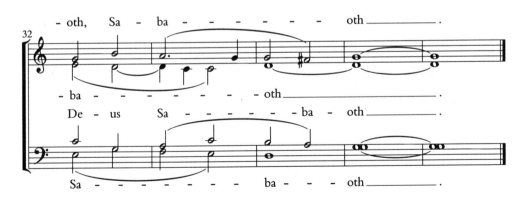

4. Richard de Bello's Song

Andante semplice ♩ = 96

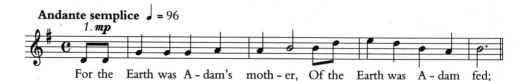

For the Earth was A – dam's moth – er, Of the Earth was A – dam fed;

And I ween, tho' man she bare here, Yet still was Earth a maid.

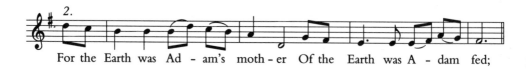

For the Earth was Ad – am's moth – er Of the Earth was A – dam fed;

And I ween, tho' man she bare here, Yet still was Earth a maid.

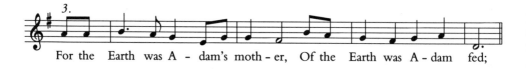

For the Earth was A – dam's moth – er, Of the Earth was A – dam fed;

And I ween, tho' man she bare here___, Yet still was Earth a maid.

2. Till the spear-like Cain thrust earthwards,
   Turning grassy green to red;
   Then I ween, that mother's tear fell,
   On Abel's silent bed.

3. But the eye of that dear mother
   Will shine like one new wed;
   When our hearts like spears of Earth-love
   Into Heaven, sun-like, spread.

5. When Springtime Comes Again

When spring - time comes a - gain, The

Now _____ heark - en how

Where dang - ling wil - lows dressed a -

All

shades of night dis - pel - ling, Sings my heart the East - er

lamb - bleat bles - ses hill and dale, How broods of fluf - fy East - er

new by lake - side dwel - ling While springs of East - er

fear _____ of wint -er quel - ling; Fresh with the East - er

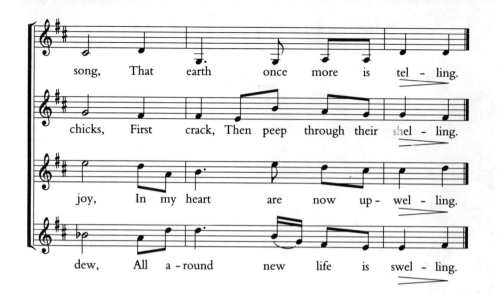

song, That earth once more is tel - ling.

chicks, First crack, Then peep through their shel - ling.

joy, In my heart are now up - wel - ling.

dew, All a - round new life is swel - ling.

6. Summer Round

Allegro aperto ♩. = 92

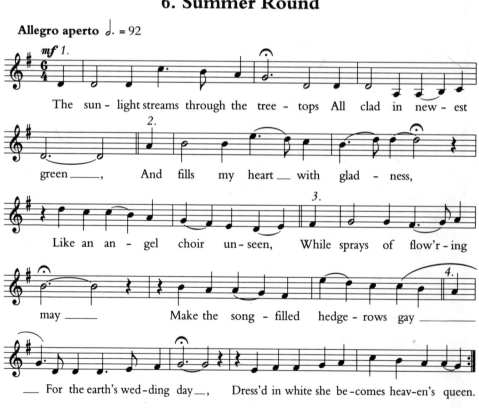

The sun - light streams through the tree - tops All clad in new - est

green ____, And fills my heart ___ with glad - ness,

Like an an - gel choir un - seen, While sprays of flow'r - ing

may ____ Make the song - filled hedge - rows gay ____

____ For the earth's wed - ding day __, Dress'd in white she be - comes heav - en's queen.

18

Two-part Songs

With upper descant

7. La Petite Fille – Shepherd on the Hillside

Allegro giocoso ♩ = 132

Descant / **Melody**

Shep - herd on the hill - side_____ pip - ing,
Quand j'é - tais pe - ti - te_____ fil - le,

Tra - la - la - la - la - la - la; Shep - herd on the
Quand j'é - tais pe -

hill - side pip - ing All a - round_____, his nibbl - ing
ti - te fil - le, J'al - lais gard - er les mou -

All a - round his nibbl - ing
J'al - lais gard - er les mou -

sheep_____, All a - round_____, his nibbl - ing sheep_____.
tons_____, J'al - lais gard - er les mou - tons _____.

sheep, All a - round his nibbl - ing sheep.
tons, J'al - lais gard - er les mou - tons.

19

2. J'étais si petite fille,
J'ai oublié mon déjeuner.

2. Sun and tummy told him it was midday,
Time to have a nibble, too.

3. Le valet de chez mon père,
Est venu me l'apporter.

3. Tragedy! His bag was empty,
High and low in vain he searched.

4. Qu'm'en voulez-vous que j'déjeune
Mes moutons sont égarés.

4. Worse to come! the flock had wandered,
Sagging smock and scattered flock.

5. On se mit à la recherche,
Mes moutons sont retrouvés.

5. Puffing up the slope came wifeling,
Saved the day with bite and sup.

6. Au son de la cornemuse,
Les moutons sont rassemblés.

6. First he primed the droning bagpipe,
Till the flock were back in sight.

7. Elle en était si joyeuse,
Qu'ell' s'en est mise à danser.

7. After crunch and munch, back to business,
Took himself and crook in hand.

8. The Twinkling Stars – Weißt du, wieviel Sternlein stehen?

Andantino ♩ = 80

mp

1. How ma - ny twink-ling stars _____ the
How ma - ny clouds are sail - ing the

mp

1. Can you say how ma - ny twinkl-ing stars, With their
Can you say how ma - ny clouds there are Sail - ing

night _____ im - bue?
wel - kin blue?

più forte

In heav - en,

light the night im - bue?
o'er the wel - kin blue?

più forte

In heav'n each one is

In heav - en, Both great-est and least, both great and

tend - ed with care and ra - diance splen - did: Both the

dim.

least, In heav - en In heav - en both great - est and least.

dim.

great - est and the least, Both the great-est and the least.

2. Can you say how many insects play
In their swarms at eventide?
Can you say how many scaly fish
In the sparkling waters glide?
In heaven each one has its number,
Be it waking or in slumber:
Both the greatest and the least,
Both the greatest and the least.

Descant:

How many insects play at eventide?
How many scaly fish in the waters glide?
In heaven . . .

1. Weißt du, wieviel Sternlein stehen
An dem blauen Himmelszelt?
Weißt du, wieviel Wolken gehen
Weit hin über alle Welt?
Gott der Herr hat sie gezählet,
Das ihm auch nicht eines fehlet
An der ganzen großen Zahl,
An der ganzen großen Zahl.

2. Weißt du, wieviel Mücklein spielen
In der hellen Sonnenglut,
Wieviel Fischlein auch sich kühlen
In der hellen Wasserflut?
Gott der Herr rief sie mit Namen,
Daß sie all ins Leben kamen,
Daß sie nun so fröhlich sind,
Daß sie nun so fröhlich sind.

Descant:

Wieviel Sternlein stehen an dem
Himmelszelt?
Wieviel Wolken gehen über aller Welt?

Gott der Herr . . .

21

9. Past Three o'Clock

One, two three four five six sev'n eight nine ten 'lev-en, 'till the

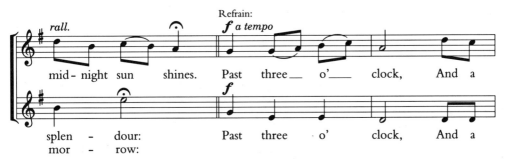

In child so ten - der, Sun's ra - diant
Mid - night's dark sor - row, Breaks with sun's

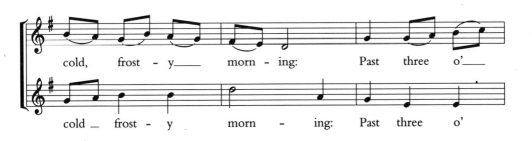

rall. **Refrain:** *f a tempo*

mid - night sun shines. Past three__ o'__ clock, And a

f

splen - dour: Past three · o' clock, And a
mor - row:

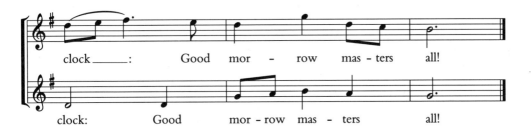

cold, frost - y__ morn - ing: Past three o'__

cold __ frost - y morn - ing: Past three o'

clock ____ : Good mor - row mas - ters all!

clock: Good mor - row mas - ters all!

10. Doña Blanca

Allegretto bucolico ♩ = 100

mf

Do-ña Blan-ca_es-tá cu - bier - ta Con pi - la - res de_o-ro y

mf

1. Do - ña Blan - ca with her hus-band Go-ing down the High Street
2. Do - ña Hedge-hog with her hus-band Go-ing through the mead-ow

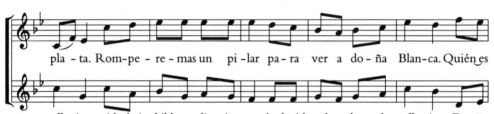

pla - ta. Rom-pe - re - mas un pi -lar pa - ra ver a do - ña Blan-ca. Quién_es

walk -ing with their child-ren cling-ing on, And with ev'- ry-bo - dy talk - ing; Do-ña
trot - ting, With their ba - bies all in line, Or in brist-ly cush-ions squat-ting; Do-ña

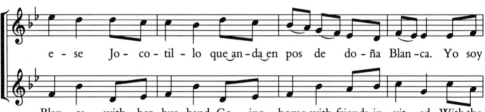

e - se Jo - co - til - lo que_an-da_en pos de do - ña Blan-ca. Yo soy

Blan - ca with her hus-band Go - ing home with friends in - vit - ed, With the
Leg - horn, through the farm-yard, with her brood of chicks all go - ing, While at

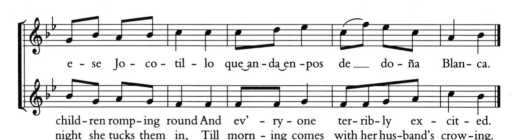

e - se Jo - co - til - lo que_an-da_en -pos de ___ do - ña Blan- ca.

child-ren romp-ing round And ev' - ry-one ter-rib-ly ex - cit - ed.
night she tucks them in, Till morn - ing comes with her hus-band's crow-ing.

11. Londonderry Air

Larghetto molto cantabile ♪ = 108

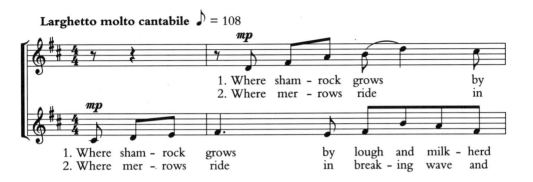

1. Where sham - rock grows by
2. Where mer - rows ride in

1. Where sham - rock grows by lough and milk - herd
2. Where mer - rows ride in break - ing wave and

lough and milk - herd mead - ow Where moun - tain side slopes
break - ing wave and sea - spray, Where gold - en gorse in

mead - ow, Where moun - tain - side slopes steep - ly to the
sea - spray, Where gold - en gorse in cush - ions scents the

steep - ly to the sea, __ Where tow' - ring peak and
cush - ions scents the air, __ Where circl - ed cross, its

sea, Where tow'r - ing peak and shel - tered vale to-
air, Where cir - cled cross, its gran - ite laced with

7

shel – tered vale to – ge – ther _____
gran – ite laced with lich – en _____

geth – er Are clad in sun and
lich – en Is soft and spark – ling

8

Are clad in sun and show'r, my mind is
Is soft with spark – ling dew: My spi – rit's

shower and green: my mind is
in the dew: my spi – rit's

9

[Refrain] *mf*

free. Where air is mild, come win- ter or come
fair.

[Refrain] *mf*

free. Where air is mild, come win – ter or come
fair.

11

sum – mer Where trout and pike in ___ drow-sy

sum – mer, Where trout and pike in drow-sy wa-ters

wa - ters dart, Where rol - ling, rol - ling moor - land 'neath the

dart, Where rol - ling moor - land, 'neath the cloud - swept

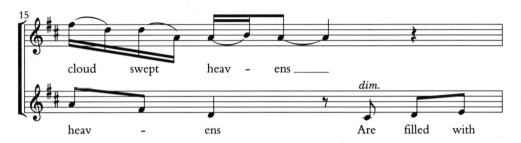

cloud swept heav - ens

heav - ens Are filled with

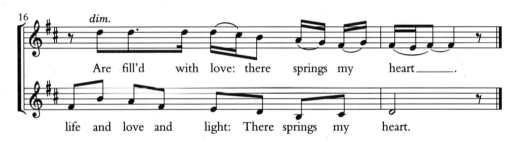

Are fill'd with love: there springs my heart.

life and love and light: There springs my heart.

1. Where shamrock grows by lough and milk-herd meadow,
   Where mountain-side slopes steeply to the sea,
   Where tow'ring peak and sheltered vale together
   Are clad in sun and show'r and green:
          My mind is free.

2. Where merrows ride in breaking wave and sea-spray,
   Where golden gorse in cushions scents the air,
   Where circled cross, its granite laced with lichen
   Is soft and sparkling in the dew:
          My spirit's fair.

Where air is mild, come winter or come summer,
Where trout and pike in drowsy waters dart,
Where rolling moorland, 'neath the cloud-swept heavens
Are filled with life and love and light:
       There springs my heart.

Part-Songs for Two Voices

12. Die Blümelein - Evensong

Bed - time comes once more for sleep - y heads.

Bed - time comes once more_____ for sleep - y heads.

1. Die Blümelein, sie schlafen schon längst im Mondenschein,
   Sie nicken mit dem Köpfchen auf ihren Stengelein.
   Es rüttelt sich der Blütenbaum,
   Er säuselt wie im Traum:
   Schlafe, schlafe, schlafe du mein Kindlein, schlaf ein!

2. Die Vögelein, sie sangen so süß im Sonnenschein,
   Sie sind zur Ruh gegangen in ihre Nestchen klein,
   Das Heimchen in den Ährengrund,
   Es tut allein sich kund:
   Schlafe, schlafe, schlafe du mein Kindlein, schlaf ein!

3. Sandmännchen kommt geschlichen und guckt durchs Fensterlein,
   Ob irgend noch ein Liebchen nicht mag zu Bette sein,
   Und wo er noch ein Kindchen fand,
   Streut er ins Aug ihm Sand:
   Schlafe, schlafe, schlafe du mein Kindlein, schlaf ein!

2. In bush and in each tree-top,
   To roost where they belong,
   All birds, on wing returning,
   Have sung their evensong;
   Beneath the stars, each feathered nest
   Is wrapped in silent rest:
   Sleep now!
   Bed-time comes once more for sleepy heads.

13. El Sol y la Luna – The Sun and the Moon

Allegretto lusingando ♩ = 116

1. Sun in the sky__, Lo-ren-zo was his name, And by
   El sol se lla-ma Lo-ren-zo, ti-bi-tón, Y la

1. Sun in the sky__, Lo-ren-zo was his name, Ti-bi ti-bi-
   El sol se lla-ma Lo-ren-zo, ti-bi-tón, Ti-bi, ti-bi-

night, the moon, Ca-ta-li-na_____: They were
lu-na Ca-ta-li-na_____: An-dan

-ton; And by night, the moon, Ca-ta-li-na: They were
-tón; Y la lu-na Ca-ta-li-na; An-dan

al-ways se-pa-ra-ted Through the fam-'ly
siem-pre se-pa-ra-dos Por dis-gus-tos

al-ways se-pa-ra-ted Through the
siem-pre se-pa-ra-dos Por dis-

feud which was rag-ing. Danc-ing ti-bi ti-bi ti-bi, ti-bi ti-bi-
de fa was mi-lia. Con el ti-bi ti-bi, ti-bi ti-bi-

fam-'ly feud which was rag-ing. Dance ti-bi ti-bi-
gus-tos de fa-mi-lia. Con el ti-bi-

- ton ___, Danc-ing ti - bi ti - bi ti - bi, ti - bi ti - bi - ton.
- tón ___, Con ___ el ___ ti - bi ti - bi, ti - bi ti - bi - tón.

- ton ___, Danc - ing ti - bi ti - bi ti - bi - ton.
- tón ___, Con ___ el ti - bi ti - bi ti - bi - tón.

1. Sun in the sky, Lorenzo was his name,
   Tibi tibiton,
   And by night, the moon, Catalina:
   They were always separated
   Through the fam'ly feud which was raging.
   Dancing tibi tibiton,
   Dancing tibi tibi tibiton.

2. "Listen to me," said Lorenzo in his pride,
   "Though you think yourself such a beauty,
   You have only me to thank."
   "I don't care two hoots," said Catalina.
   Dancing tibi ...

3. "And, while I'm at it, see here," said
       Catalina,
   "You're a scorching, blistering nuisance:
   Burning deserts, drying rivers ..."
   "Just shut up," Lorenzo interrupted.
   Dancing tibi ...

4. "You with your light leading bandits in
       the night:
   I wouldn't touch you with a barge-pole."
   "Sir," she answered, "nobody asked you:
   Stick to the day, and keep your distance!"
   Dancing tibi ...

5. High from the zenith the stars looked down,
   "We will tell you a secret;" they twinkled,
   "Life needs both the night and day-time,
   From the tundra to the equator."
   Dancing tibi ...

2. El sol le dijo a la luna: tibitón,
   No presumas demasiado,
   Que el vestido con que luces
   De limosna te lo han dado.
   Con el tibitón ...

3. El sol le dijo a la luna: tibitón,
   No quiero nada contigo;
   Pasas la noche en la calle
   Con ladrones y bandidos.
   Con el tibitón ...

14. Gentil Coqu'licot – Fluttering Poppies

Andante semplice ♩ = 108

mf / *p*

1. When in my gar - den   one fine day,   When in my
1. J'ai des-cen-du   dans   mon jar - din,   J'ai des-cen-

When in my gar - den one fine day,
J'ai des-cen-du dans mon jar-din,

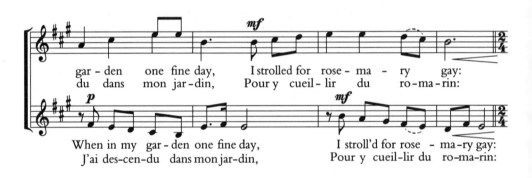

gar - den   one fine day,   I strolled for rose - ma - ry   gay:
du dans   mon jar - din,   Pour y cueil - lir   du   ro - ma - rin:

When in my gar - den one fine day,
J'ai des-cen-du dans mon jar-din,

I stroll'd for rose - ma-ry gay:
Pour y cueil-lir du ro-ma-rin:

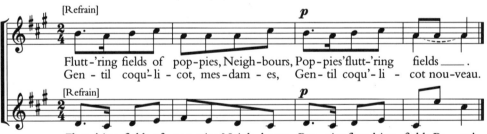

[Refrain]   *p*

Flutt-'ring fields of pop-pies, Neigh-bours, Pop-pies'flutt-'ring   fields ____ .
Gen - til coqu'-li - cot, mes-dam - es,   Gen - til coqu'-li - cot nou-veau.

[Refrain]   *p*

Flutt-'ring fields of pop-pies, Neigh-bours, Pop-pies flutt-'ring fields Pa - pa!
Gen - til coqu'-li - cot, mes-dam - es,   Gen - til coqu'-li - cot nou-veau.

2. Pour y cueillir du romarin,
Pour y cueillir du romarin,
   J'n'en avais pas cueilli trois brins.
     Gentil coqu'licot ...

3. J'n'en avais pas cueilli trois brins,
J'n'en avais pas cueilli trois brins,
   Qu'un rossignol vint sur ma main.
     Gentil coqu'licot ...

4. Qu'un rossignol vint sur ma main,
Qu'un rossignol vint sur ma main,
   Il me dit trois mots en latin.
     Gentil coqu'licot ...

5. Il me dit trois mots en latin,
Il me dit trois mots en latin,
   Que les hommes ne valent rien.
     Gentil coqu'licot ...

6. Que les hommes ne valent rien,
Que les hommes ne valent rien,
   Et les garçons encor bien moins.
     Gentil coqu'licot ...

1. When in my garden one fine day,
When in my garden one fine day,
   I strolled for rosemary gay:
     Flutt'ring fields of poppies
     Neighbours
     Poppies' flutt'ring fields. Papa!

2. I strolled for rosemary gay,
I strolled for rosemary gay,
   There hopped a bright-feathered jay;
     Flutt'ring fields ...

3. There hopped a bright-feathered jay,
There hopped a bright-feathered jay,
   To me in secret to say:
     Flutt'ring fields ...

4. To me in secret to say,
To me in secret to say,
   Whene'er from home you do stray:
     Flutt'ring fields ...

5. Whene'er from home you do stray,
Whene'er from home you do stray,
   Then please remember, I pray:
     Flutt'ring fields ...

6. Then please remember, I pray,
Then please remember, I pray,
   Your deepest heart to obey:
     Flutt'ring fields ...

7. Your deepest heart to obey,
Your deepest heart to obey,
   And so ends this roundelay.
     Flutt'ring fields ...

15. Canción del Pandero - Tambourine Song

Allegro agitato ♩ = 92

Cas - ta - net and tam - bou - ri - no
Call to all the peo - ple with their

1. Cas - ta - net and tam - bou - ri - no, Cas - ta - net and tam - bou - ri - no
   Call to all the peo - ple with their

Call a - loud to all the peo - ple; Ai - la - la, la - la - la - la - la____
In - vi - ta - tion to the dance.

Call a - loud to all the peo - ple_____;
In - vi - ta - tion to the dance_____.

1. Ai - la - la - la - la, ____,
   Cas - ta - net and tam - bou - ri - no

2. Ai - la____ la, Ai -
   Laced man - til - las, Pom - pons bob - bing,

cresc.
- la - la, Ai - la - la, Ai - la - la, Ai - la
Silk sa - shes swish - ing; Ai - la - la - la, la - la - la - la____

34

Ai - la - la, la - la - la - la - la.   TAMBOURINES

Ai - la   CASTANETS

Este pandero que toco
Tiene lengua_y sabe_hablar,
Tiene lengua_y sabe_hablar,
Y con ella_está diciendo:
Salgan mozos a bailar,
Salgan mozos a bailar.
      Ai-la-la-la, Ai-la-la-la,
      Ai-la-la-la-la,
      Ai-la-la-la,
      Ai-la-la-la.

2. Knuckles knocking, jingles clatt'ring,
    Knuckles knocking, jingles clatt'ring,
     Call aloud to all the people;
    Knuckles knocking, jingles clatt'ring
     Call to …

3. Clacking heels and snapping fingers,
    Clacking heels and snapping fingers,
     Call aloud to all the people;
    Clacking heels and snapping fingers,
     Call to …

16. Le Chant du Coucou – As I Wandered

Allegro assai ♩ = 144

mp

1. As I wand-er'd through a cop-pice Where the cuck-oo
1. En pas-sant dans un p'tit bois, Où le cou-cou chant-

sang, yes where the cuck-oo sang, The spar-rows scat-ter'd at his
-ait. Où le cou-cou chant-ait; Dans son jo-li chant il di-

cresc.

twang: Cuck-oo, cuck-oo, cuck-oo, cuck-oo; But as for me I thought he
-sait: Cou-cou, cou-cou, cou-cou, cou-cou, Et moi qui croy-ais qu'il di-

sang: They're af-ter you, They're af-ter you! And so a-
-sait: Cass' lui le cou, cass'-lui le cou! Et moi de

- way   spa - ra - spa - ra - spa and so a - way   I   sprang.

m'en   cou' cou' cou' cou' cour' Et moi de   m'en cour - ir.

2. As I wandered past a duck-pond
   Where the ducks all quacked,
   Yes, where the ducks all quacked,
   In puddles paddling, proudly packed:
   "Quack quack, quack quack, quack quack, quack quack;"
   But as for me, I thought they clacked:
   "Let him be whacked,
   Let him be whacked:"
   And so away
   Ta-ra-ta-ra-ta
   And so away I tracked.

3. By a water mill I wandered
   Where the wheel turned round,
   Yes, where the wheel turned round,
   The golden grain it gladly ground:
   "From harvest field to baker-browned;"
   But as for me, I heard the sound:
   "We'll have him drowned,
   We'll have him drowned:"
   So off I bounced
   Ba-ra-ba-ra-ba
   So off I bounced with a bound.

Part-Songs for Three Voices

Descant, soprano, alto

17. Sobre las Pajas – Basque Lullaby

Lento piacevole ♪ = 96

1. Peace - ful as sleep! Babe in the man - ger; Shep - herds
1. Dul - ce Be - lén! Guar - das la per - la del E -

kneel - ing, Hearts a - glow: Gifts they bring to greet the
- dén____ Dul - ce Be - lén! Bril - la tu noch - e con ful -

child: Snow - white lamb - fleece, fine as silk,____ Fresh cut
- gor. Del cie - lo tie - nes el re - splen - dor. Flu - yen tus

whis - tle, Sweet warm milk;____ Peace - ful as sleep!
cam - pos hoy de dul - zor: Dul - ce Be - lén!

Peace - ful as sleep!

38

2. Peaceful as sleep! Babe in the manger;
Oxen bowing
By his side:
Joseph lifts the lantern bright:
    Pure and humble, rich yet poor,
Shepherds waiting,
    Open door;
        Peaceful as sleep!

3. Peaceful as sleep! Babe in the manger;
Choirs of angels
Fill the air;
Round the crib they throng in light:
    Darkness of night shall turn to day
When at the heart,
    That child doth lay;
        Peaceful as sleep!

18. Sheep may Safely Graze - Schafe können sicher weiden

Andante pastorale ♩ = 52

Shin - ing sun or dark - 'ning storm cloud, con - stant is a shep-herd's care; By his flock in quiet grove pas-tur'd, Or bar - ren moun -tain heights, Where rag-ing temp -est smites,

39

care, his own soul a - bid - ing; In his task he finds con - tent - ment: Feed - ing, fend - ing, Guard - ing, tend - ing; For his sheep _____ his life he'll dare.

p cresc.

mf

Dal segno al fine

19. Sans Day Carol

And Ma-ry bore Je-sus Christ, Our sav-iour for to be; And the

The

And the

silk:
cross:
all:
dead:

first tree in the green-wood, it was the hol - ly. Hol - ly, hol -

first tree in the green-wood, it was the hol - ly. Hol -

first tree in the green-wood, it was the hol - ly Hol -

-ly _____, The _ first tree in the wood was the ho (o)l-ly.

-ly, And the first tree in the green-wood it was the hol - ly.

-ly _____, It _ was the hol - ly.

20. Still, Still, Still

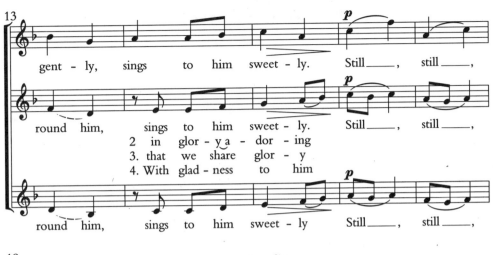

gent - ly, sings to him sweet - ly. Still____, still____,

round him, sings to him sweet - ly. Still____, still____,
2 in glor - y a - dor - ing
3. that we share glor - y
4. With glad - ness to him

round him, sings to him sweet - ly Still____, still____,

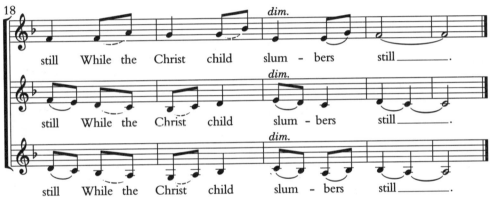

still While the Christ child slum - bers still____.

still While the Christ child slum - bers still____.

still While the Christ child slum - bers still____.

1. Still, still, still, weils Kindlein schlafen will.
Die Englein tun schön jubilieren,
Bei dem Kripplein musizieren.
Still, still, still, weils Kindlein schlafen will.

2. Schlaf, schlaf, schlaf, mein liebes Kindlein schlaf!
Die Mutter tut es niedersingen,
Ihre große Lieb' darbringen.
Schlaf, schlaf, schlaf, mein liebes Kindlein schlaf!

2. Sleep, sleep, sleep,
O gold of heaven, now sleep!
Around him cluster hosts of angels,
Chanting their songs, in glory adoring.
Sleep, sleep, sleep …

3. Great, great, great,
Is the light that shines on earth;
For God hath left the heavens' high throne,
On earth to dwell, for Man to share glory.
Great, great, great …

4. Come, come, come,
Thou love of the World now come,
Draw near, all ye people, worship before him;
Open your hearts with gladness to him:
Come, come, come …

45

21. Trio from the Magic Flute

The sky, a-wash with sun-rise splen-dour, Glows

ra-diant in the east; All threats of sor-row cower and

va-nish, As night her hold has ceased; When

Part-Songs for Three Mixed Voices

Two treble and one male voice

22. 'Twas on a Monday Morning

* hanging, ironing, airing, folding, weaving

2. 'Twas on a Tuesday morning,
   A-wringing of her linen-o

3. 'Twas on a Wednesday morning,
   A-hanging ...

4. 'Twas on a Thursday morning,
   An-ironing ...

5. 'Twas on a Friday morning,
   An-airing ...

6. 'Twas on a Saturday morning,
   A-folding ...

7. 'Twas on a Sunday morning,
   A-wearing ...

49

23. Hebridean Cradle Song

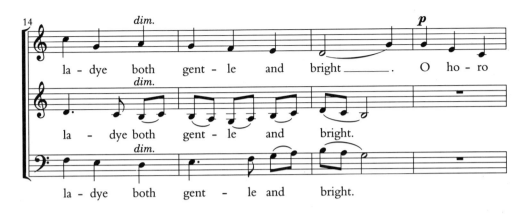

24. The Seven Joys of Mary

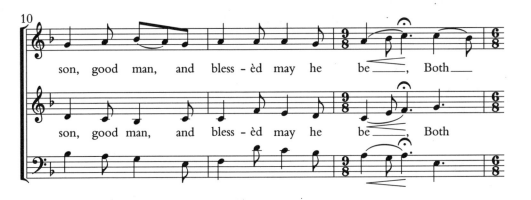

son, good man, and bless - èd may he be___, Both___

son, good man, and bless - èd may he be___, Both

Fa - ther, Son and Ho - ly Ghost, To all e - ter - ni - ty___.

Fa - ther, Son and Ho - ly Ghost, To all e - ter - ni - ty___.

2. The next good joy that Mary had,
   It was the joy of two;
   To see her own son, Jesus Christ,
   To make the lame to go:
      To make the lame to go ...

3. The next good joy that Mary had,
   It was the joy of three;
   To see her own son, Jesus Christ,
   To make the blind to see:
      To make the blind to see ...

4. The next good joy that Mary had,
   It was the joy of four;
   To see her own son, Jesus Christ,
   To read the bible o'er;
      To read the bible o'er ...

5. The next good joy that Mary had,
   It was the joy of five;
   To see her own son, Jesus Christ,
   To bring the dead alive:
      To bring the dead alive ...

6. The next good joy that Mary had,
   It was the joy of six;
   To see her own son, Jesus Christ,
   Upon the crucifix;
      Upon the crucifix ...

7. The next good joy that Mary had,
   It was the joy of seven;
   To see her own son, Jesus Christ,
   To wear the crown of heaven:
      To wear the crown ...

25. Dancing Day

Con mosso ♩ = 132

To - mor - row shall be_____ my danc - ing

day: I would my true____ love did____ so

chance____ To see_____ the____ le - gend of____ my

play, To call my true love to my dance: Sing

play, To call my true love to the dance:

Sing O my

play,

O my love, O my love, my love, my

O sing, my love, sing O sing my

love, my love , O sing, sing my

love; This have I done for my true love.

love; This have I done for my true love .

love. This have I done for my true love .

2. For thirty pence Judas me sold,
   His covetousness for to advance;
   "Mark whom I kiss, the same do hold,"
   This same is he shall lead the dance:
       Sing O …

3. Before Pilate the crown me brought,
   Where Barabbas had deliverance;
   They scourged me and set me at nought,
   Judged me to die to lead the dance:
       Sing O …

4. Then on the cross hanged I was,
   Where a spear to my heart did glance;
   There issued forth both water and blood,
   To call my true love to my dance:
       Sing O …

5. And as the sun in chariot gold,
   Was dulled, like knight unhorsed by lance,
   The earth did quake, the rocks were rent
   Beneath the trembling of the dance:
       Sing O …

6. Then down to hell I took my way
   For my true love's deliverance,
   And rose again on the third day,
   Up to my true love and the dance:
       Sing O …

7. With spices rare they came at morn
   But stood amazed as in a trance,
   When they beheld the stone rolled back,
   To set me free to lead the dance:
       Sing O …

8. In raiment white my angel stood,
   Like lightning was his countenance,
   Whereat the keepers shook with fear,
   Dead to my true love and the dance:
       Sing O …

9. Then in the garden I appeared
   My love's new dawning to enhance;
   In upper room, on sandy shore
   I led the gathering Easter dance:
       Sing O …

10. Then up to heaven I did ascend,
    Where now I dwell in sure substance
    On the right hand of God, that Man
    May come unto the general dance:
        Sing O …

26. The Mantle of St John

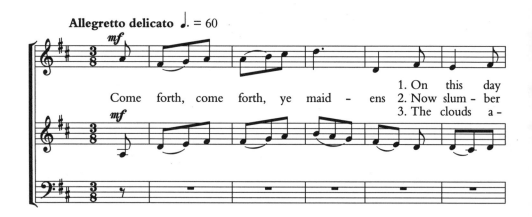

Allegretto delicato ♩. = 60

Come forth, come forth, ye maid - ens
1. On this day
2. Now slum - ber
3. The clouds a -

6

of __ St John _____, It is the Bap - tist's
not __ a - way _____, The high - heav'n, sun - filled
way __ have roll'd _____, The fields of wheat are

The man - tle of __ St John _____

11

morn - ing (♪) that breaks __ the hills __ up - on _____
morn - ing of the Ho - ly Bap - tist's day _____
rip'n - ing in height __ of sum - mer's gold _____

_____ on the Bap - tist's Day, Morn - ing

16

__; So let us go forth __ to - geth - er while the bless - èd
__; There's tre - foil in the mead - ow And there's li - lies
__; The jas - mine and the ros - es, In an air of

breaks __ the hills up - on the man - tle of __ the Bap -

57

day   is   new_____,   To   dress   with   flow'rs   the
on   the   lea _____,   And   haw - thorn   blos - soms
mant - led   peace_____;   We'll   weave   in   gar - lands

dress   with   flow'rs_____
blos- soms   clus -
gar - lands_____

tist,   The   man - tle   of   the   Bap -

cresc.

snow - white   we - ther,   ere   the   sun   hath   dried_____
clus - ter'd   white   which   you   may   pluck   a - long_____
on   the   brow_____   of   the   ram   with   whit -

cresc.

___ snow-white   we - ther,   e'er   the   sun ___ hath   dried ___ the
tered   white,_____   you   may   pluck   a - long   with
___ on   the   brow, _____   of   the   ram   with   whit - est

cresc.

- tist's   Day;   Come   forth   the   day   of   the

_____ the   dew_____   .
_____ with   me_____   .
_____ est   fleece_____   .

dew,   the   sun ___ hath   dried ___ the   dew_____   .
me,   may   pluck___   a - long___   with   me_____   .
fleece,   the   ram ___ with   whit - est   fleece_____   .

Bap - tist,   for   the   man - tle   of   St   John

58

27. Maria im Dornwald - The Flowering Thornwood

Poco mezzo voce ♩ = 69

As Ma-ry, walk'd through thick-et wild_ Ky-ri-e e-lei-

As Ma-ry, walk'd through thick-et wild_ Ky-ri-e e-lei-son

-son; Be-reft of leaf and bird and song, That

Ky-ri-e e-lei - son_____, Ky - ri

thorn-torn wood-land for sev'n years long_: Je-sus ex Ma-ri - a.

e, Ky - ri - e____, Je-sus ex Ma-ri - a.

1. Maria durch ein Dornwald ging,
   Kyrie eleison!
   Maria durch ein Dornwald ging,
   Der hat in sieben Jahr kein Laub getragen.
   Jesus und Maria.

2. Was trug Maria unter ihrem Herz'n?
   Kyrie eleison!
   Ein kleines Kindlein ohne Schmerz'n,
   Das trug Maria unter ihrem Herzen.
   Jesus und Maria.

3. Da haben die Dornen Rosen geschlag'n.
   Kyrie eleison!
   Als das Kindlein durch den Wald getrag'n,
   Da haben die Dornen Rosen getragen.
   Jesus und Maria.

[*English versese 2 & 3 over*]

59

2. Thus Mary waited for her child;
   Kyrie Eleison:
   The thoughts she pondered in her heart
   Bridg'd heaven and earth, so long apart:
   Jesus ex Maria.

3. At that, the wintry wind turn'd mild;
   Kyrie Eleison:
   New joy and life around her sprung,
   Red roses sweet, the thorns among;
   Jesus ex Maria.

28. Paradise Carol

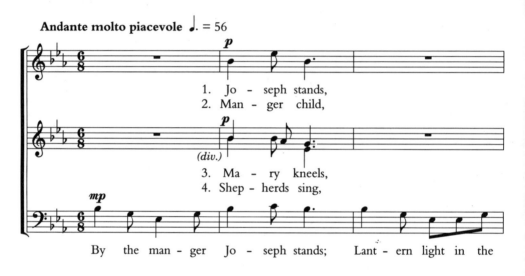

she sings,

Sings the moth - er Ma - ry. The

mf The

(div.)

sings the moth - er Ma - ry. The Bells of Pa - ra - dise

mf

The Bells of Pa - ra - dise rang _____ that

mf

Bells of Pa - ra - dise rang that night, That night _____,

Bells _____ of Pa - ra - dise _____ rang __ that night,

rang that night, A - cross the a - ges dark and wild;

night _____.

Shep - herds

pp

pp

mp

(div.)

Shep - herds heard them and sped to greet the mid - night child:

heard the Bells of Pa - ra - dise so mild ___ *mp* That

Gift of heav - en, Hope he brings and

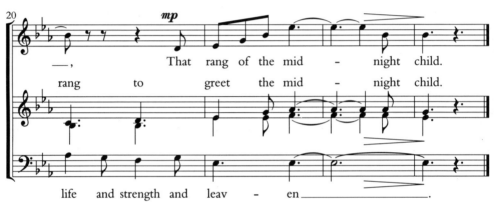

___, That rang of the mid - night child.

rang to greet the mid - night child.

life and strength and leav - en ___.

2. In the manger lies the child,
   Warming hearts with his message mild;
   Born of God, he is undefiled,
   Of Paradise,
   So sings the mother Mary …

3. By the manger Mary kneels,
   Joy within her heart she feels;
   Wounds of the world, her child, he heals
   Through Paradise,
   So sings the mother Mary …

4. Rocking the manger, shepherds sing;
   From pure hearts, their offering;
   In a new way the child will bring
   To Paradise
   All those who sing with Mary …

Part-Songs for Three Mixed Voices

Treble, tenor, bass

29. Three Kings of Orient

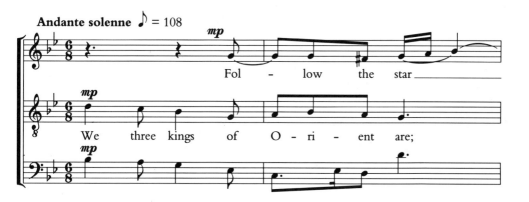

- low ___ the star ___.
still pro-ceed-ing, Guide us to thy per-fect light.

2. *Radiant the star, ...*
   Born a king on Bethlehem's plain,
   Gold I bring, to crown him again
   King for ever, ceasing never,
   Over us all to reign:
       O star ...

3. *Worship the star, ...*
   Frankincense to offer have I;
   Incense owns a deity nigh:
   Prayer and praising, all men raising,
   Worship him, God most high:
       O star ...

4. *Guiding, the star, ...*
   Myrrh is mine; its bitter perfume
   Breathes a life of gathering gloom;
   Sorrowing, sighing, bleeding dying,
   Sealed in a stone cold tomb:
       O star ...

5. *Glorious the star, ...*
   Glorious now, behold him arise,
   King and God, and sacrifice
   Heav'n sings alleluia,
   Alleluia, the earth replies:
       O star ...

30. St Patrick's Breastplate

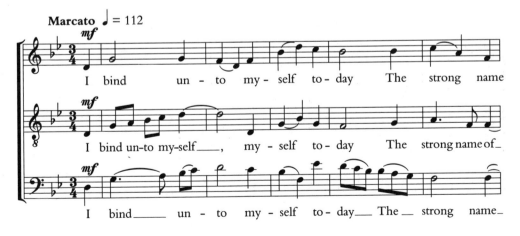

Marcato ♩ = 112
mf

I bind un-to my-self to-day The strong name

mf
I bind un-to my-self___, my-self to-day The strong name of___

mf
I bind___ un-to my-self to-day___ The ___ strong name___

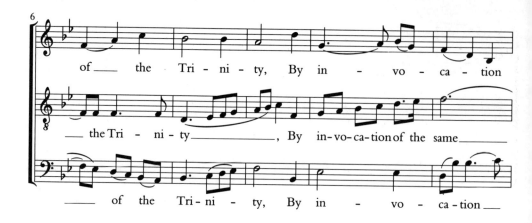

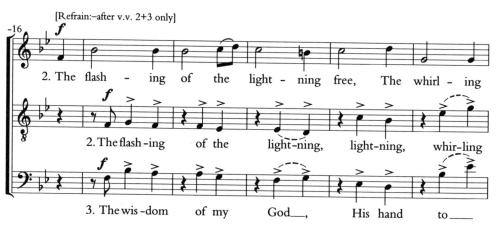

66

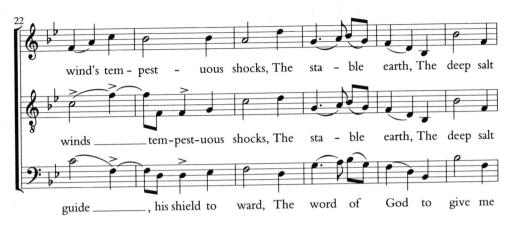

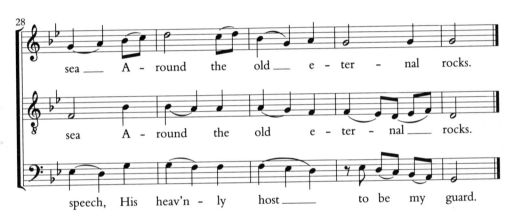

2. I bind unto myself today
   The virtues of the star-lit heaven,
   The glorious sun's life-giving ray,
   The whiteness of the moon at even;
   The flashing of the lightning free,
   The whirling wind's tempestuous shocks,
   The stable earth, and deep salt sea,
   Around the old eternal rocks.

3. I bind unto myself today
   The power of God to hold and lead,
   His eye to see, his might to stay,
   His ear to hearken to my need.
   The wisdom of my God to teach,
   His hand to guide, his shield to ward;
   The word of God to give me speech,
   His heav'nly host to be my guard.

31. As I Walked out one May Morning

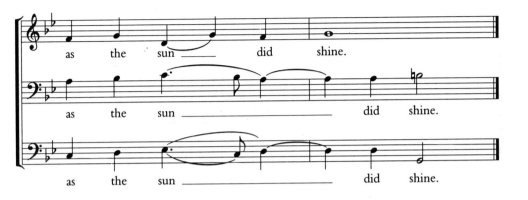

as the sun ____ did shine.

as the sun _____ did shine.

as the sun _____ did shine.

2. "What makes you rise so soon, my dear,
   Your journey to pursue?
   Your pretty little feet, they tread so sweet,
   Strike off the morning dew."

3. "I'm going to feed my father's flock,
   His young and tender lambs,
   That over hills and over dales
   Lie waiting for their dams."

4. "O stay, O stay! You handsome maid,
   And rest a moment here,
   For there is none but you alone
   That I do love so dear.

5. "How gloriously the sun doth shine,
   How pleasant is the air;
   I'd rather rest on a true love's breast
   Than any other where.

6. "For I am thine, and thou art mine,
   No man shall uncomfort thee;
   We'll join our hands in wedded bands,
   And a-married we will be."

Part-Songs for Two Voices

Treble and male

32. Zacchaeus and the Sycamore Tree

In Je - ri - cho it was, In Jor - dan's val - ley

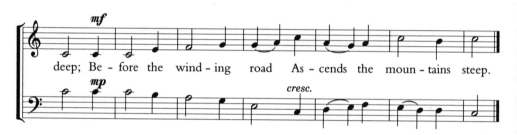

deep; Be - fore the wind - ing road As - cends the moun - tains steep.

2. The streets were thick with crowds
   Around Zacchaeus' inn;
   But though his purse was full
   His heart was sore with sin.

3. A sycamore he climbed,
   Above the thronging heads;
   And waited midst the leaves
   Where light its glory sheds.

4. And as the Lord came by,
   The beauty in his eyes
   He raised towards the shade,
   Beneath the sun-filled skies.

5. "Zacchaeus, come below
   To welcome me as guest
   For in your heart I'll lodge
   To bring you joy and rest."

70

33. Lifelong

Cantabile ma quasi extempore ♩ = 76

[Verses 2–5 over]

2. When I was a youth the earth seemed hard:
   Rock and wave and wind they bruised and pierced,
   Rain and hail brought drenching to life and limb;
   When …

3. When I was a man the earth seemed steep:
   Yet, at every climb, a way I found,
   Rain in mountain spring my life's chalice brimmed;
   When …

4. When my hair grew white the earth seemed old:
   Fruit and shrivelled seed were rich in store,
   Rain or shine sailed peacefully through each day;
   When …

5. When I lay at death the earth shone bright:
   Star and sun and love streamed from her heart,
   Borne by wings unfailing, I touched her crown;
   When …

Part-Songs for Three Mixed Voices

Either soprano, alto, male, or treble, tenor, bass

34. The Blacksmith

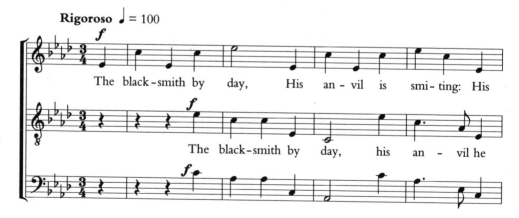

The black-smith by day, His an-vil is smi-ting: His

The black-smith by day, his an-vil he

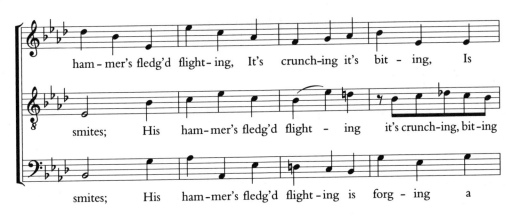

ham-mer's fledg'd flight-ing, It's crunch-ing it's bit - ing, Is

smites; His ham-mer's fledg'd flight - ing it's crunch-ing, bit-ing

smites; His ham-mer's fledg'd flight-ing is forg - ing a

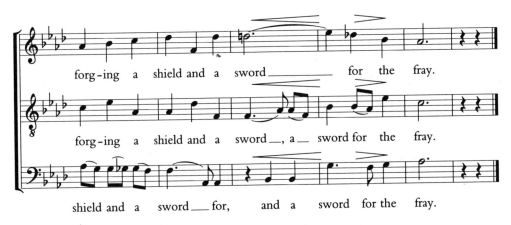

forg-ing a shield and a sword_____ for the fray.

forg-ing a shield and a sword__, a__ sword for the fray.

shield and a sword__ for, and a sword for the fray.

2. By night the sky's gleam,
   The meteor sparks whirling,
   Their iron thrusts are hurling,
   Their warning unfurling,
   Bids darkness melt back
      in the sun's glorious ray.

3. In cavernous glare,
   The dragon's gloat flashing,
   His jaws fiercely gnashing,
   His flail-spiked tail's lashing;
   He churns slime and smoke
      in his sulphurous bay.

4. Knight Michaël rides,
   His steel never failing,
   In starry stream trailing,
   Man's weakness assailing:
   His height be my shaft!
      His stern glance light my way!

35. Philomel

Allegro facile ♩ = 126

When the earth with spring re - turn - ing, Vests her -

And the glade and leaf - y thick - ets Are ar -

When a sweet - er

- self___ in fresh - er sheen, When ___ a

- rayed in liv - ing green. When a sweet - er

frag - rance breath - eth, Flow' - ry fields and vales a -

cresc.

frag - rance breath - eth, Flow'-ry fields and vales a -

frag - rance breath - eth, Flow' - ry fields and vales a -

★*Ossia* If fancied, this run may
lead into a long held D:

Two or three of the sopranos (or tenors) should suffice.

2. Night and day, from bush and greenwood,
Sweeter than an earthly lyre,
She, unwearied songstress, carols,
Distancing the feathered quire;
In her airy flight ascending
To the summit of the tree,
Thence full fain she trills her mellow
Canticles of festal glee.

3. Fills the hillside, fills the valley,
Bids the groves and thickets ring,
Made indeed exceeding glorious
Through the joyousness of spring.
None could teach such heavenly music,
None implant such tuneful skill,
Save the king of realms celestial,
Who doth all things at his will.

Part-Songs for Mixed Choir

Soprano, alto, tenor, bass

36. Sankt Michaels Lied

Sonore e risoluto ♩ = 84

1. Un - con - quered he - ro of the skies, Saint Mi - cha - ël; A - gainst the foe with us a - rise, Thine aid we pray___, The

foe to slay____, Saint Mi - cha - ël.

1. Unüberwindlich starker Held,
   Sankt Michael!
Komm uns zur Hilf, zieh mit ins Feld!
   Hilf uns hie kämpfen, die Feinde dämpfen,
      Sankt Michael!

2. Du bist der himmlich Bannerherr,
   Sankt Michael!
Die Engel sind dein Königsheer.
   Hilf uns ...

3. O starker Held, groß ist dein Kraft,
   Sankt Michael!
Ach komm mit deiner Ritterschaft!
   Hilf uns ...

2. The heavenly banner thou dost bear, Saint Michaël;
The angels do thine armour wear;
   Thine aid ...

3. Great is thy might, strong is thy hand, Saint Michaël!
Great o'er the sea, great o'er the land;
   Thine aid ...

37. Ride the Waves of Life

Moderato ma sempre energico $\quad \flat = 96$

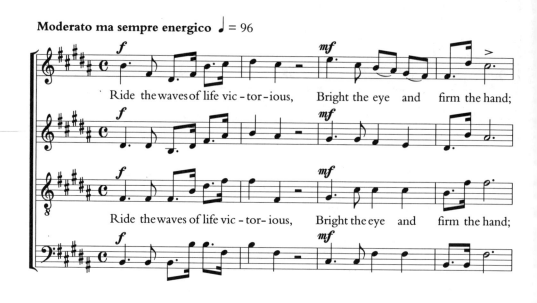

Ride the waves of life vic-tor-ious, Bright the eye and firm the hand;

Ride the waves of life vic-tor-ious, Bright the eye and firm the hand;

Fill the sails of hope with glad-ness, Bring the car-go safe to land.

Fill the sails of hope with glad-ness, Bring the car-go safe to land.

When the ship be-gins to shud-der At the tem - pest dark and

When the ship be-gins to shud-der at the tem - pest

drear; When the threat'-ning storm clouds thun-der Time to cast a-way your

drear; When the threat'-ning storm-clouds thun-der Time to cast a-way your

fear, Time to cast a - way your fear. Ride the waves of life vic-

fear, Time to cast a - way your fear. Ride the waves of life vic-

- tor- ious, Bright the eye and firm the hand; Fill the sails of hope with

- tor- ious, Bright the eye and firm the hand; Fill the sails of hope with

glad-ness, Ba - nish doubt and hold your stand. Know Le-vi-a-than is

pow'r - less If you steer your chart - ed course; Keep the flame of life a -

pow'r - less If you steer your chart - ed course; Keep the flame of life a -

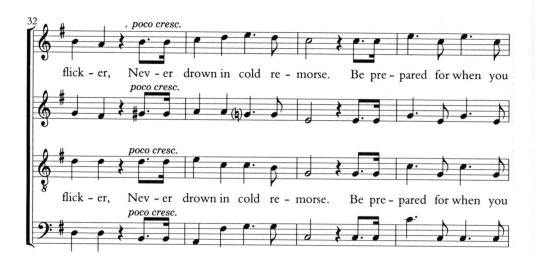

flick - er, Nev - er drown in cold re - morse. Be pre - pared for when you

flick - er, Nev - er drown in cold re - morse. Be pre - pared for when you

jour - ney Neath the tro - pics blaz - ing breath; Be a - lert e - quipp'd and

jour - ney Neath the tro - pics blaz - ing breath; Be a - lert e - quipp'd and

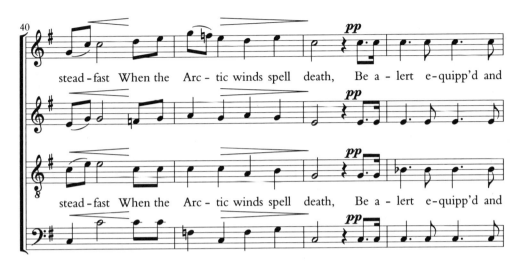

stead-fast When the Arc - tic winds spell death, Be a - lert e-quipp'd and

stead-fast When the Arc - tic winds spell death, Be a - lert e-quipp'd and

stead - fast When the Arc-tic winds spell death, When the Arc-tic winds spell death.

stead - fast When the Arc-tic winds spell death, When the Arc-tic winds spell death.

38. Es ist ein Ros' entsprungen

Es ist ein Ros' ent - sprung - en Aus ein - er Wurz - el zart.
Als uns die Alt - en sung - en Aus Jes - se kam die Art;

A rose of wond-rous beau - ty, In high - est heav'n un folds.
Its pet-als deep red vel - vet Its scent God's sec - ret holds;

Und hat ein Blüm - lein bracht____,

Of flow'rs it is the queen

Mitt - en im kalt - en Win - ter Wohl zu der hal - ben Nacht.

And decks that roy - al gar - den With full - est bliss se - rene.

84

87

29

Und hat ein Blüm - lein bracht_____.
Of flow'rs it is ____ the queen_____.

bracht, Und____ hat ein Blüm-lein bracht.
queen, Of____ flow'rs it is the____ queen.

____ hat ein Blüm-lein bracht_____.
____ flow'rs it is the queen_____.

Mit - ten im
And decks that

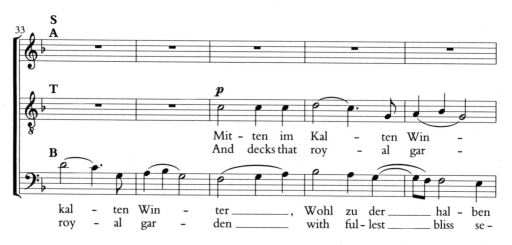

33 S A

T

Mit - ten im Kal - ten Win -
And decks that roy - al gar -

B

kal - ten Win - ter_____, Wohl zu der_____ hal - ben
roy - al gar - den_____ with ful - lest_____ bliss se -

2. Das Röslein das ich meine,
Davon Esias sagt,
Hat uns gebracht alleine
Marie die reine Magd.
Aus Gottes ew'gem Rat
Hat sie ein Kind geboren,
Wohl zu der halben Nacht.

2. This rose is sprung from Jesse,
Maria is her name;
Her son's birth, deep in winter
A new day shall proclaim;
'Tis sunrise: time to start
And tender that fair blossom
In garden of the heart.

39. I Saw Three Ships

Tempo comodo ♩. = 92/100

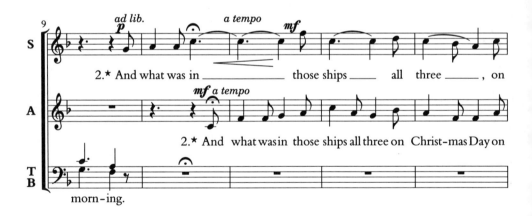

★ Male voices sing verses 1, 3, 5, 7; female voices sing verses 2, 4, 6, 8.

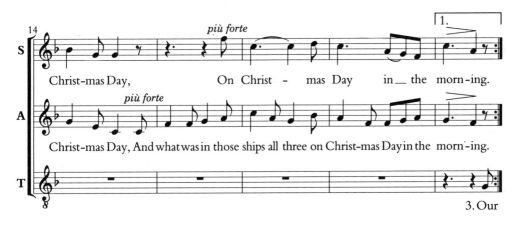

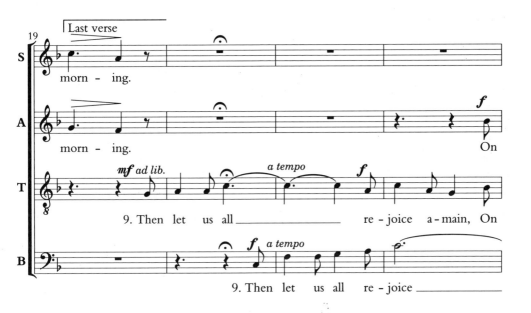

[★. . .★]This passage may be cut in which case ignore the
fact that the last phrase begins at the end of a $\frac{3}{8}$ bar.

2. And what was in those ships all three? *On . . .*
3. Our Saviour Christ and his lady. *On . . .*
4. Pray, whither sailed those ships all three. *On . . .*
5. O they sailed into Bethlehem. *On . . .*
6. And all the bells on earth shall ring. *On . . .*
7. And all the angels in heaven shall sing. *On . . .*
8. And all the souls on earth shall sing. *On . . .*

93

40. Passiontide Carol from the Odenwald

Piangevole ♩ = 84

S: O Son, dear-est Son, O dear-est Je-su mine,

A / A: What will be-come of thee on___ Sun - day?
2. Mon - day?

Quasi allargando

T / B:
1. On Sun - day___ I shall be king___ and decked in
roy - al robes and strewn___, strewn___ with palms.

2. On Mon - day___ shall I be a wan - der - er, "for___ the
Son of man hath no - where to___ lay his Head."

3. On Tues - day___ shall I be the pro - phet tel - ling the

★ The dynamics should suit the content of the words throughout.

world that "Heav'n and Earth_____ shall_____ pass a - way."

4. On Wedn's - day_____ shall I be en - humb - led and sold for

thir - ty sil - ver pie - ces by_____ one I love.

5. On Thurs - day_____ shall I be the Lamb_____ up - on the

tab - le of the Pass - o -ver, of_____ Pass - o - ver.

6. O Moth - er_____ my dear - est Moth - er, ask not of

Fri - day till it is come be - fore thine eyes.

7. On Sa - tur - day_____ a seed of corn shall I be, the life of

heav'n re - born in earth_____, Earth's new Sun.

41. Chorus from Telemann's St Luke's Passion

Now sor - row wrings the heart___with grief! Sor - row, sor-

Now sor - row wrings the heart with grief! Sor - row, sor-

Now sor - row wrings the heart with grief! Sor -

- row, now! Now sor - row wrings the heart___with grief!

- row, now! Now sor - row wrings the heart with grief!

- row, Now sor - row wrings the heart with grief!

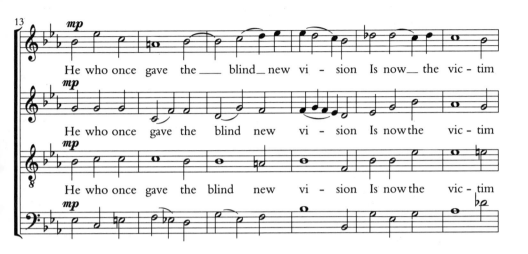

He who once gave the ___ blind ___ new vi - sion Is now ___ the vic - tim

He who once gave the blind new vi - sion Is now the vic - tim

He who once gave the blind new vi - sion Is now the vic - tim

of ___ de - ri - sion; Thorn-press'd, Thorn-press'd his king - ly reign ___ so

of de - ri - sion; Thorn-press'd, Thorn-press'd his king - ly reign so

brief. Oh sor - row wrings the heart ___ with grief! Sor - row, sor-

brief. Oh sor - row wrings the heart with grief! Sor - row, sor-

Sor -

- row, now! Now sor-row wrings the heart ___ with grief! He whose salt

- row, now! Now sor-row wrings the heart with grief! He whose salt

- row, Now sor-row wrings the heart with grief! He whose salt

tears __ for all peo - ple __ were __ flow - ing, Now with his cross __ to

tears for all were flow - ing, Now with his cross to

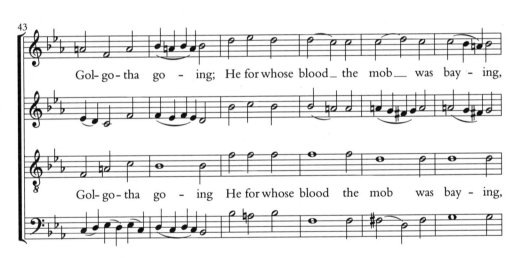

Gol-go-tha go — ing; He for whose blood __ the mob __ was bay - ing,

Gol-go-tha go — ing He for whose blood the mob was bay - ing,

For their for - give - ness now __ is pray-ing, Nailed to __ the __ tree with-out

Nailed, Nailed __ to __ the __

For their for - give - ness now __ is pray-ing, Nailed to the tree, nailed

life __ nor __ leaf __, to the tree, to __ the tree with-out life or

tree, nailed __ to __ the __ tree __ With - out life __ or

to the tree __, to the tree with - out __ life or

to the tree, the tree, with - out __ life __ or

leaf. Such sor-row wrings the heart with grief! Sor - row, sor - row, now!

leaf. Such sor-row wrings the heart with grief! Sor - row, sor - row, now!

leaf. Such sor-row wrings the heart with grief! Sor - row, sor - row, now!

leaf. Such sor-row wrings the heart with grief! Sor - row sor - row now!

Now sor-row wrings the heart with grief_____, with grief.

Now sor-row wrings the heart with grief_____, with grief.

Now sor-row wrings the heart with grief, wrings the heart with grief.

Now sor-row wrings the heart with grief, wrings the heart with grief.

42. Sacred Song

Sor - row can - not hold me, Then __ de - vo - tion __, joy and love __ en -
With its ten - der pow - ers Pen - e - tra - ting all like gen - tle __

can - not hold me, Joy and love _____ en -
ten - der pow - ers Pen - e - tra - ting

can - not hold me, Joy and love en -
ten - der pow - ers Pen - e - tra - ting

can - not hold me, Joy _____ and love en - fold __
ten - der pow - ers Pen - e - tra - ting __

fold _____ me.
show - ers.

fold me, Then de - vo - tion joy __ and love en - fold __ me. __
all _____, Pen - e - tra - ting all __ like gen - tle __ show - ers.

fold me, Then de - vo - tion, and love en - fold me.
all like gen - tle gen - tle gen - tle show - ers.

me, Then de - vo - tion, love en - fold _____ me.
all, Pen - e - tra - ting all like gen - tle show'rs.

103

43. The Sun in Easter Rising

Con moto ♩ = 120

The sun in Eas-ter splen-dour bright Out

Out

strides the shades of___ each dark night, Death's bonds of

strides the shades___ of each dark night, Death's bonds of
Death's bonds of___

strides the shades of each dark night, Death's bonds of

sor-row break - ing,

sor-row break - ing, Joy-ful hearts mak - - - -
___ sor-row break - ing,

sor-row break - ing, Joy-ful hearts mak - - - -

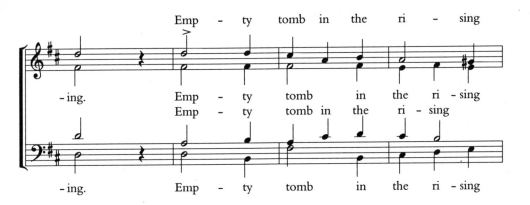

2. With joy of heaven resounding near,
   The gates of death can hold no fear;
   Fresh life is freely flowing,
   Strength in each heart bestowing.
   Empty tomb ...

3. So sing the triumph of our Lord:
   The word made flesh; the flesh made word;
   Made word with spirit winging;
   Earth like a star up-springing.
   Empty tomb ...

44. Midsummer Day

Delicato ma vivace ♪ = 152

1. Wel - come Mid - sum - mer Day _____,
2. Mid - day o - ver head _____,
3. Then in the west ____ ar - rayed _____,
4. Friends full of dance ____ and song _____,

[ALTO] *mf* cresc.

1. (Sun ____ in the ra - diant
2. (Sun ____ in the heights of
3. (Sun ____ in the glow - ing
4. (Sun ____ in ____ thank - ful

1. On this mid - sum - mer morn - ing _____
2. It will as - cend ____ vic - to - rious _____
3. Red - dened gold it ____ will lin - ger _____
4. Hands ____ and smiles ____ u - ni - ting _____

All the...

1. east.) All the moun - tains a - dorn - ing ____, To
2. heav'n.) Ma - king earth ____ more glo - rious ____, Her
3. west.) Joy of the feast ____, the bring - er ____; And
4. hearts.) Hands and smiles ____ u - nit - ing ____, With

— ,
— ,
— ,
— ,

1. Mid - sum - mer morn - ing __,
2. The earth ____ more glor - ious __,
3. The feast ____ joy bring - ing __,
4. By hand ____ u - ni - ted __,

1. greet both man and beast _____ , For
2. flow - ers in car - pets spread _____ , To
3. flames that rise and fade _____ ; Of
4. glis - ten - ing light___ so strong_____ . And

1. The moun - tains a - dorn - ing,
2. Her flow - ers in car - pets,
3. As flames___ are ris - ing,
4. In strong___ light glist'n - ing,

1. this hap - py feast___, For this hap - py feast___.
2. sum - mer___ wed___, To sum - mer___ wed___.
3. sun fire __ is made___, Of sun fire__ is made___.
4. day - light___ long___, And day - light___ long___.

feast_____,This Mid -sum - mer Day.

1. For this hap - py feast,
2. To sum - mer___ wed, } This Mid - sum - mer Day___.
3. Of sun fire__ is made,
4. And day - light___ long,

45. Tuba Mirum

111

46. Psalm 105

Largamente ♩ = 60

f

1. Thank ye the Lord on His high Throne, And praise His ho - ly name;____
Sing un-to Him a song of praise And spread His won-drous fame;____

f

2. To Ab-ra - ham, His ser-vant wise, His cov-en-ant He gave:____
Ja - cob and I - saac, and their seed, For e - ver, He would save;____

mf

1. Good - ness and strength Flow from His hand; He at the end of

mf

2. So on Mount Si - nai Mos - es bore Tab - lets of stone from

time will stand; His cho-sen folk He____ then will claim.

which the law Deep in their hearts He did en - grave.

113

114

47. So Beauty on the Waters Stood

And_____ then a mo - tion_____ he them taught That_____

And then a mo - tion he them_____ taught That_____

And then a mo - tion he them taught That_____

And then a mo - tion he them taught That_____

___ eld - er than him - self_____ was thought;

___ eld - er than him - self was thought;

___ eld - er than_____ him - self_____ was thought; Which

___ eld - er than him - self was thought; Which

117

48. Can you Make me a Cambric Shirt?

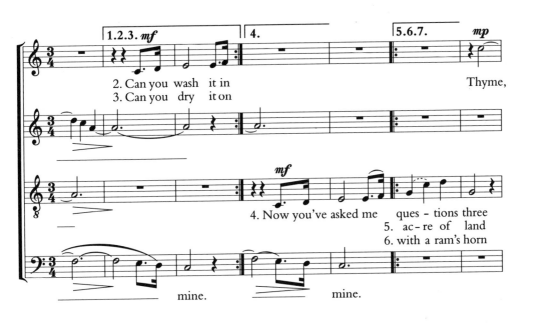

2. Can you wash it in
3. Can you dry it on

Thyme,

mine.

mine.

4. Now you've asked me   ques - tions three
5.   ac - re of   land
6. with a ram's horn

pars   -   ley, sage and rose-ma-ry

Thyme and pars -ley   sage ____   and rose - ma-ry

4. I   hope __ you'll
5. Be - tween the salt
6. And   saw it all

7.

Can you be a true lov-er of mine?
of _____ mine _____.
of mine _____.
mine _____. Can you be a true lov-er of mine?

2. Can you wash it in yonder well
   Which never sprang water, nor rain ever fell?
   Parsley, sage, rosemary and thyme;
   And you will be a true lover,
   true lover of mine, lover of mine.

3. Can you dry it on yonder thorn
   Which never bore blossom since Adam was born?
   Parsley ...

4. Now you have asked me questions three,
   I hope you'll answer as many for me.
   Parsley ...

5. Can you find me an acre of land
   Between the salt water and the sea-sand?
   Parsley ...

6. Can you plough it with a ram's horn
   And sow it all over with one pepper corn?
   Parsley ...

7. Can you reap it with a sickle of leath'r
   And bind it up with a peacock's feather?
   Parsley ...

121

49. Ecce Sacerdos

★ The square brackets indicate when the trombones play in the original version.

qui in di - e - bus su - is

su - is, qui in di - e - bus su - is, qui in di-

e - bus su - is, qui in di - e - bus

qui in di - e - bus su - is, qui in di-

qui in di - e- bus su-is pla - cu -it De - o.

e - bus su - is pla - cu -it De - o.

su -is, qui in di - e-bus su-is pla - cu-it De - o.

e - bus su - is pla - cu-it De - o

fe - cit il - lum Do - mi - nus cres - ce - re in ple-bem su - am, in ple-bem

fe - cit il - lum Do - mi - nus cres - ce - re in ple-bem su - am, in ple-bem

fe - cit il - lum Do - mi - nus cres - ce - re in ple-bem su - am, in ple-bem

fe - cit il - lum Do - mi - nus cres - ce - re in ple-bem su - am, in ple-bem

su - am, in ple - bem su - am, in ple - bem su - am.

su - am, in ple - bem su - am, in ple - bem su - am.

su - am, in ple - bem su - am, in ple - bem su - am.

su - am, in ple - bem su - am, in ple - bem su - am.

[– .]

50. Santa Luccia

Espressivo ♪ = 69

Here on the wa - ters
Heave of the oars - man,

Bathed in the moon - light,
Wist - ful his bar - ca - rolle,

Here on the wa - ters,
Heave of the oars - men,

Bathed in the moon - light,
Wist - ful his bar - ca - rolle,

Ze - phyrs stir soft - ly,
Tear - ful his me - mo - ries,

Waves gent - ly lap - ping;
His soul en - wrap - ping:

Ze - phyrs stir soft - ly,
Tear - ful his me - mo - ries,

Waves gent - ly lap - ping;
His soul en - wrap - ping:

2. Closed many a brother's eye,
   Drowned neath a stormy sky;
   Stirred by the seagull's cry,
   Mem'ries are welling;
   His eye remaining bright,
   Beyond death, his steadfast sight;

There, where her guiding light,
Dark fear is quelling:
   Yet never doubting,
Hope ever sprouting;
   Santa Luccia, Santa Luccia.

Choral Pieces for more than Four Voices

51. The Destruction of Senacherib

Impetuoso ♩ = 112/120

sempre forte

1. The As - sy - rian came down
2. For the an - gel of death
3. With the dew on his brow

sempre forte

1. The As - sy - rian came down like a wolf on the fold,

[TENOR] *sempre forte*

And his

like a wolf on the fold
spread his wings on the blast,
and the rust on his mail

And the sheen of their
And their hearts but once
And the lan - ces up-

And the sheen of their spears was like

co-horts were gleam - ing in pur - ple and gold;

spears was like stars ___,   like   stars ___,   like   stars,
heaved and for ev - er   stood   still ___,   stood   still,
lift - ed the trum-pet   un - blown ___,   un - blown,

Night on

stars   on the sea,   Night on

when the   blue wave rolls night -ly on deep Ga-li-lee

deep Ga - li - lee _____,

Night on deep Ga-li-lee.   Like the leaves of
And the foam of
And the i - dols

deep Ga - li - lee,   Night on   deep   Ga-li -   lee.

Like the leaves of the fo - rest when

the fo - rest, When sum - mer is green,
his gas - ping lay white on the turf
are broke in the tem - ple of Baal,

sum - mer is green, That host with their ban - ners at sun - set was seen; Like the

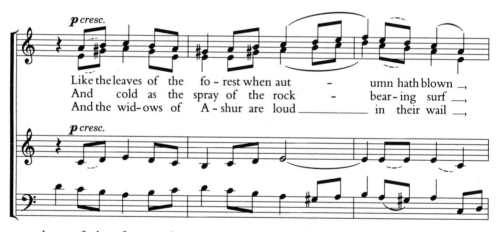

Like the leaves of the fo - rest when aut - umn hath blown _,
And cold as the spray of the rock - bear - ing surf __,
And the wid - ows of A - shur are loud in their wail _,

leaves of the fo - rest when aut - umn hath blown, That host on the mor - row lay

pause last time only

They lay with-er'd and strewn. They lay with - er'd and strewn.

pause last time only

They lay with - er'd and strewn.

with-ered and strewn, They lay with-er'd and strewn. They lay with - er'd and strewn.

with-er'd and strewn, They lay with - - - er'd and strewn.

pause last time only

2. For the angel of death spread his wings on the blast,
   And breathed in the face of the foe as he passed;
   And the eyes of the sleepers waxed deadly and chill,
   And their hearts but once heaved and for ever stood still.

   And there lay the steed with his nostril all wide,
   And through it there rolled not the breath of his pride;
   And the foam of his gasping lay white on the turf,
   And cold as the spray of the rock-beating surf.

3. And there lay the rider distorted and pale,
   With the dew on his brow and the rust on his mail;
   And tents were all silent, the banners alone,
   The lances uplifted, the trumpet unblown.

   And the widows of Ashur are loud in their wail,
   And the idols are broke in the temple of Baal;
   And the Might of the Gentile, unsmote by the sword,
   Hath melted like snow in the glance of the Lord.

52. Sing we and Chant it

Now is best lei - sure, To take our plea - sure. Fa la
Let spare no trea - sure, To live in plea - sure.

Now is best lei - sure, To take our plea - sure.
Let spare no trea - sure, To live in plea - sure. Fa la la la la la la

Now is best lei - sure, To take our plea - sure. Fa la la la,
Let spare no trea - sure, To live in plea - sure.

Now is best lei - sure, To take our plea - sure. Fa la la la la
Let spare no trea - sure, To live in plea - sure.

Fa la la la la la la

(2nd. time f) **1.** **2.**

la la la la, fa la la la la. la

(2nd. time f)
la, fa la la la, fa la la la. la.

(2nd. time f)
fa la la la la la, la la la, fa la la la. la.

(2nd. time f)
la la, fa la la la la la, fa la la la la. la.

(2nd. time f) *f*
la, fa la la la la la, fa la la. la.

133

53. Song for Mothering Day

Andante piacevole ♩ = 144

[Solo] *mf*

[Choir] *mp*

There grew in Heav'n a Lin-den Tree, there grew in Heav'n a Lin-den

tree,

With fair - est

[Solo] *mf*

p

There grew in Heav'n a Lin - den tree,

p

blos - som la - den; With fair - est blos - som la -

[Choir] *mp*

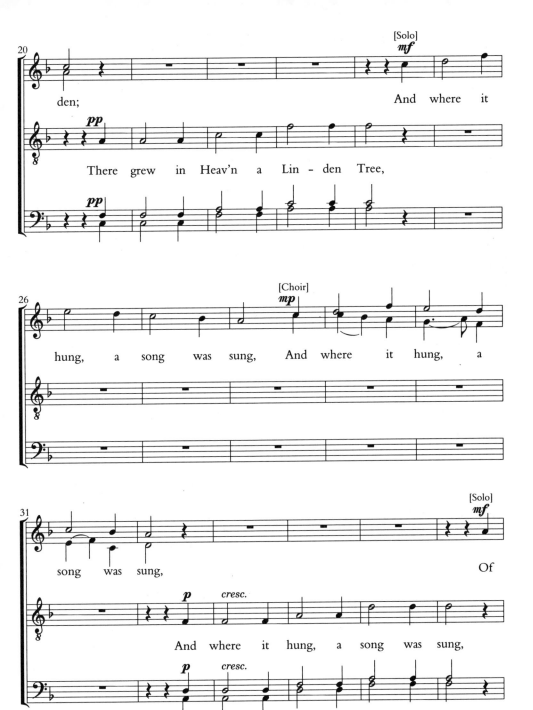

[Choir]

praise for a fair mai - den. Of praise for a fair mai -

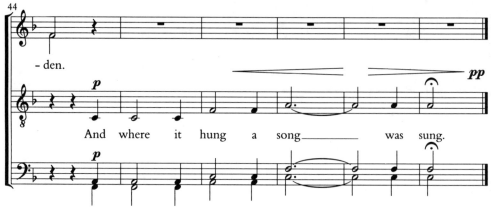

- den.

And where it hung a song_____ was sung.

2. "My Gabriel," quoth God the Lord,
   Of messengers the fairest,
   "Go, tell that maid, 'Be not afraid;
   The Son of God thou barest'."

3. With lily white he greeted her:
   "O thou, of maids, the chosen,
   Thou shalt give birth when dark the earth
   And winter fields are frozen."

4. So, when the winter darkness grew,
   Along with many a stranger,
   From Nazareth she made her way
   To Bethle'm's humble manger.

5. And in her heart a song she heard -
   The song of Eden's garden:
   Through Adam's sweat the earth must yield
   E'er God that fruit shall pardon.

6. And pains of labour shall attend
   Each birth, as Cain and Abel
   Were born to Eve; yet time will turn
   With thy son, born in stable.

7. Throughout that birth, when dark the night,
   Her heart sang like no other:
   'Twas Gabriel and his Linden song
   Of praise for earth's sweet Mother.

Notes

1. Dona Nobis Pacem
To the well-known round for three voices has been added an extra part (in the bass clef). This is intended to help a choir "warm up." Female voices can sing the three-part round, continuing while male voices sing lines 4, 5 and 6 (the extra part); or vice versa. It is also possible to sing the whole piece as a six-part round.

2. Michaelmas Song
If sung by an adult choir, it may be more accommodating to transpose this down a tone into C minor. A strong point should be made of the contrast between the outer impetus of the 6/8 tempo and the more inward vigour of the frequent duplets.

3. Sanctus
This is a movement from Palestrina's (1525–95) *Missa ad Fugam* of 1555, the year in which Pope Julius III had admitted him to the Sistine Chapel in St Peter's, Rome. The parts are in canon.

4. Richard de Bello's Song
The words of this song were written to celebrate the opening of a new building at the Hereford Waldorf School. The inspiration for the song was taken from the World Map (Mappa Mundi), a treasure from the Middle Ages, kept in Hereford Cathedral. The map was made *c.* 1290 by Richard de Bello of Lincoln, after whom the song is entitled.

5. When Springtime Comes Again
This round of Haydn's (1732–1809) is characterized harmonically by its forthright modulation to the dominant halfway through each line, and melodically by the distinctive contours of each of its four lines. The pace should be particularly leisurely at its two feminine cadences, so that each may be smoothly rounded off.

6. Summer Round
When and if each voice repeats the melody of the round, the first note (on "The") should be reduced to a quaver.

7. La Petite Fille/Shepherd on the Hillside
The melody and words of this song may well have been learnt in the younger language classes. The descant here printed may be added when the song is taken up again in Classes 4 or 5. The "cornemuse," referred to in the French version, is principally thought of as a peasant-played bagpipe, though there were also refined versions used by the upper classes.

The tune's insistence on three bar phrases supports the song's home-spun, bucolic nature.

8. The Twinkling Stars/Weißt du, wieviel Sternlein stehen
A folk melody from Baden. The brackets round the words in verse two indicate which words should be omitted by the descant voice.

9. Past Three o'Clock
This traditional tune comes from an old collection entitled "London Waits." It conjures up three different meanings of the word: the earliest type of wait was a town watchman; it was also the name given to town musicians in the seventeenth century, who often played in the streets at night or for ceremonious occasions — two or three shawms and a sackbut; later, in the nineteenth century, carol singers (and players) were also colloquially referred to as waits.

10. Doña Blanca

The comically swaggering alternation of this song's 3/4 and 2/4 passages should be thoroughly savoured. The original is probably known in Spanish speaking countries as a ring game. Here it is included because of the fresh and jaunty lilt of its rhythm.

11. Londonderry Air

County Derry (named Londonderry by the English) is in the north of Ireland, having associations, through Lough Foil, with the Children of Lir — amongst the most poignant of Irish stories; and with Columba, one of the most approachable of saints. This tune, with its breadth and heart-felt climax, is in the finest tradition of Irish melody. If it is not being accompanied by recorders, a sympathetic key to sing in would be D flat (in which case the first note should be C natural).

"Merrows" (verse 2) is an Irish word for undines, water spirits.

12. Die Blümelein/Evensong

Well known both in its original folk-song form and as Brahms' arrangement for voice and piano (entitled Sandmännchen), this song evokes the peaceful mood of nightfall, a mood that can be attained by giving the quaver movement of the second voice as unhurried a treatment as possible — without dragging, of course.

13. El Sol y la Luna/The Sun and the Moon

Heavy weather should not be made of the imitation in the second voice of the second and fourth phrases. Nevertheless, if this is sung as an action song in language lessons, the musical point might be brought out by dressing one of the "firsts" in a sun halo and one of the "seconds" in a head-dress representing the moon.

14. Gentil Coqu'licot/Fluttering Poppies

The French words and tune are traditional. A slight ritenuto up to the last note before the 2/4 section may be advisable — but then the same quaver speed as before should be taken up immediately.

15. Canción del Pandero/Tambourine Song

The 5/4 time signature and gripping rhythm injects an ecstasy into this piece. The cross rhythms in the descant of the refrain should be sung with breadth and aplomb.

16. Le Chant du Coucou/As I Wandered

As far as possible without becoming breathless, treat this piece as a *moto perpetuo*, the crochets standing out prominently. That there are three of these at the end of the last phrase provides a sufficient, built-in buffer.

17. Sobre las Pajas/Basque Lullaby

The key of this exquisite Basque folk-song can be changed according to need. Recorders playing the tune may find the key of A major more convenient; adult altos will probably be able to sing the deeper notes caused by transposing the whole thing down into F major.

18. Sheep may Safely Graze/Schafe können sicher weiden

This immortal melody is taken from one of J.S. Bach's (1685–1750) cantatas. The original setting is for solo soprano with two flutes playing an obbligato part. The present arrangement is written in such a way that it can be sung as an unaccompanied trio or with the original accompaniment. Something of the remarkable composition technique demonstrated by Bach in the pieces he wrote for solo violin or solo cello, has been emulated in this arrangement, so that his extraordinary richness of harmony and counterpoint still comes across.

19. Sans Day Carol

Both melody and words are from Cornish oral tradition, its name deriving from St Day, the place where it was first written down.

20. Still, Still, Still

Rhythmic variants of this traditional melody from Salzburg, Mozart's birthplace, extend the opening phrase from seven to eight bars; here the seven bar version has been used to gain the inner dynamic that results, while at the same time retaining the peace and inwardness that the tune engenders.

21. Trio from The Magic Flute

The text of *The Magic Flute* has, as its cultural background, the fairy tale, ancient Egyptian ceremonial, and the deeper significance of freemasonry, all of which are clad in a light-hearted theatrical garb that easily endears itself to the eye and ear. The three boys (Genii), who sing this trio, appear as saving-grace at moments of despair or confusion several times during the opera. Mozart (1756–91) gives them music of serene simplicity, one of the outstanding achievements of his late style.

22. 'Twas on a Monday Morning

Without creating a veneer that would falsify the plain folk-like nature of this jig, all phrases will benefit from being well shaped. A busy-body pace needs to be maintained thoughout, amidst which the bass of bars 9–12, though still fun, should be felt as a pool of rhythmic calm.

23. Hebridean Cradle Song

A completely unfractured, sustained tone is necessary for this piece, the wide octave intervals being sung with unshakable assurance.

24. The Seven Joys of Mary

This was an extremely popular carol, sung in many versions — ten joys and twelve joys being later variants — all over England.

25. Dancing Day

The tempo is only a fraction less than one in a bar, necessitating superb dexterity in all parts, but especially in the bass run in bar 9. The resultant flow should be unimpeded, like a wave coming in to shore, and taking elements like the alto cross-rhythm just before the refrain in its surf-riding stride. Notwithstanding, the pause comes as a magic interruption — a voice which stills the waters as it casts its influence over the last phrase.

26. The Mantle of St John

The words of this song are derived from an old Spanish ballad relating to St John's day, June 24, in which a local custom is described.

27. Maria im Dornwald/The Flowering Thornwood

That the Madonna in a bower of roses was a precious image north of the Alps, witness paintings such as Stephan Lochner's *Marie in der Rosenlaube* or Martin Schongauer's *Madonna im Rosenhang*. This traditional song indicates that the legendary image of the transition from barren and aggressive thorn to flourishing blossom has inner significance for the soul.

28. Paradise Carol

The medieval mind easily filled the stark Bethlehem inn-stable with a host of details. One of these, evident both in art and miracle play, was of Joseph providing a simple light. In this version, the light emanating from the stable is linked with the light of Paradise, Paradise itself having connotations of inner illumination in esoteric Jewish tradition. The melody in this arrangement is given to the male voices.

29. Three Kings of Orient

This carol has won a firm place in the heritage of Christmas carols, although it was composed as recently as *c.* 1857 by Dr Hopkins of Pennsylvania. This arrangement explores the musical potential of a guiding star. The sopranos should aim for an "ethereal" tone, which nevertheless is securely in the lead.

30. St Patrick's Breastplate

As this song mingles the three elements of battle-song, invocation and affirmative belief, it will be understandable that the male-dominant tone colour of this arrangement is intentional. But it should not drown — a fault that can be avoided by the melody being strong and sustained, while the two lower parts are sung with a hint of *staccato* throughout: weathered granite contrasting with jagged limestone. Or the "apocryphal" image may be preferred — of King Leary's men (when they sallied forth to capture St Patrick in order to put him to death) mistaking both him and his followers for wild deer!

31. As I walked out one May morning

A West Country folk tune. The bar lines in this setting should be regarded very freely, particularly in the tenor and bass, where they mostly only indicate the phrasing in the traditional melody.

32. Zacchaeus and the Sycamore Tree

The well-known but comparatively little referred-to incident is related in St Luke's Gospel (19:4). This simple but telling musical setting comes from the *Piae Cantiones* of 1582. In it, unusually and fascinatingly, the two voices begin two octaves apart, coming to a unison at the end of the first phrase, the contrary motion being exactly reversed for the second phrase.

33. Lifelong

Despite its 63/4 time-signature, this piece was conceived of in folk vein. The lack of bar-line need not be an impediment if each singer keeps a wary eye on the other part.

34. The Blacksmith

Although the original poem that Brahms (1833–97) set to music has little reference to the blacksmith, the composer seized on the image of the smithy to produce a piano accompaniment that depicts, in musical terms, the sparks flying up into the cowl over the forge fire and the hefty strokes of the smith as he works at the anvil. These two elements should be borne in mind when singing both Brahms' original melody and the two accompanying voices in this arrangement, in order to produce the required flair and vitality of tone.

35. Philomel
The School of Chartres could be described as the last flowering of ancient Celtic wisdom. Its teaching went far beyond the confines of Roman sectarian dogma, the text of this spring-song by Bishop Fulbertus being a superb example. Written in 1028, it slightly pre-dates the present cathedral, which itself is a miracle of survival amongst medieval architecture, sculpture and stained glass.

36. Sankt Michaels Lied
This hymn of praise and intercession for the Feast of St Michael is taken from a German Psalter of 1642, though the text does not derive directly from one of the psalms. It has the character of Lutheran congregational psalmody and should be sung with unabashed strength and conviction.

37. Ride the Waves of Life
A genre to which Schubert (1797–1828) was very partial was that of unaccompanied male-voice chorus, it being connected with the emerging camaraderie of post-Napoleonic, Viennese society. Wine and love were prominent themes, though Schubert's music surpasses them, as the sentiment of this piece (the original here being transposed and arranged for mixed choir) well illustrates.

38. Es ist ein Ros' entsprungen
In this setting, the music of two composers is juxtaposed. Michael Praetorius' (c. 1570–1621) setting of the melody, which appeared in the *Musae Sioniae* of 1605, is of unparalleled beauty and exudes the personally contemplative spirit of the Reformation; it should be sung as a chorale with the other two sections to follow. The music of the second section is by a contemporary of Praetorius, Melchior Vulpius (c. 1570–1615). He latinized the family name: Fuchs. Motets and hymns in Protestant style were his speciality. The similarity between the opening phrase of this canon and the first line of *Es ist ein Ros'* enable it to be used in a way that anticipates tentatively the chorale prelude which was to become such an important feature of Lutheran church life in the mid-seventeenth and eighteenth centuries. (The link phrase, to the words "Und hat ein Blümlein bracht," has been written as part of this setting.)

39. I Saw Three Ships
The uplifting pulse that pervades this tune has made it justly popular. It has been preserved as part of the great heritage of folk-song for which we have to thank the tireless work of the collectors at the turn of the last century.

The wistful phrase that introduces each verse in this setting should not be allowed to interrupt the tidal flow of the melody; it might be seen as the turn of the tide, between male and female tone-colour.

40. Passiontide Carol from the Odenwald
The seven days of Holy Week — the week leading up to Easter — are characterized distinctively in this carol. The music is intended to be sung as follows: female voices (the question), male voices (the answer), female and male voices together. And so on, for each verse.

41. Chorus from Telemann's St Luke's Passion
Georg Philipp Telemann (1681-1767) was amongst the most prolific of composers. His output arose mainly because of the formal demands of the position he held in Hamburg from 1721 till his death in 1767. No fewer than 46 settings of the Passion are recorded; five of these are to texts based on St Luke's account. The present chorus bears evidence of the long tradition in northern art of the deeply personal response to and interpretation of the Passion story. Among visual artists we have Tilman Riemenschneider and Albrecht Dürer; while in music, J.S. Bach's St Matthew and St John Passions probably represent the epitome of this stream of artistic feeling.

42. Sacred Song
This song was composed in May 1819. It is one of Schubert's (1797–1828) rare settings of words by Novalis, words that display an inner religious fervour, direct from the heart and entirely free from any denominational colouring. This version for S.A.T.B. has been made from the original setting for voice and piano.

43. The Sun in Easter Rising
Johannes Eccard (1553–1611) wrote this piece in 1594. The natural rhythmic vigour of its 3/4 time is shot through with musical phrases that are free of the bar line. This should create an impression of supportive forces streaming into the centre from all directions.

44. Midsummer Day

This is a Swiss folk song. Its mood requires a leisurely tempo and an unsophisticated handling of the way that (in this arrangement) the male and female voices are dovetailed. The first soprano and the first tenor phrases are both part of the original melody.

45. Tuba Mirum

These words are well known as coming from the Requiem Mass. The setting from which this very free arrangement has been made is attributed to Joseph (1732–1809) or Michael (1737–1806) Haydn. The opening eight bars rest, indicated in square brackets, formed an introduction in the original for orchestra with viola obbligato. This arrangement offers opportunity for strong tonal contrasts in keeping with the apocalyptic nature of the words.

46. Psalm 105

Heinrich Schütz (1585–1672), the composer of this piece, was grounded in the Venetian style of composition through the tuition he received from Giovanni Gabrieli during the last four years of the master's life and regime at St Mark's. This is evidenced in the flowing lines of the Halleluias which conclude the piece, unusual in a metrical psalm setting.

47. So Beauty on the Waters stood

Alfonso Ferrabosco (c. 1578–1628), of Italian descent, was born and died in Greenwich. He is known to have played the lute at the funeral of Elizabeth I. He collaborated with Ben Jonson to produce elaborate court masques; these were usually produced at Whitehall. This piece is a four-part arrangement of a lute song, a genre in which Ferrabosco excelled and which enjoyed a short but unrivalled flowering at the turn of the sixteenth to seventeenth century.

48. Can you Make me a Cambric Shirt?

The imagery in this remarkable verse, handed down by tradition, has been discussed at some length by Martin Croes in *Journal for Anthroposophy*, Spring 1990. Access to the folk-wisdom contained in it might be via any one of its images. Croes suggests, for instance, that the "thorn" in verse three might have some connection with Joseph of Arimathea's coming to England, he being a "distinguished member of the Sanhedrin." (The Glastonbury thorn.)

Cambric is fine white linen.

49. Ecce Sacerdos

This arrangement of one of Anton Bruckner's (1824–96) motets plays on the tonal contrast between female voices and full choir. Bruckner, in accentuating some phrases by the addition of trombones, indicates something of the monumental effect of the startling harmonic changes he employs. These are fully in line with the "wildness and daring" for which he was notorious. (The Vienna Philharmonic Orchestra rejected his First Symphony, precisely on that account!)

50. Santa Luccia

This is a completely chordal setting of the traditional Neapolitan song. The choir should therefore sing as one voice, yet with all the freedom of a solo melodic line, in romantic style — which might well sport a *tenuto* on the high soprano D in the penultimate bar!

51. The Destruction of Senacherib

This setting of Byron's poem, in which the events alluded to in Isaiah 37:36 are described in impetuous fashion, was composed by Carl Loewe (1796–1869) in 1825. The wide-ranging melody (typical of his songs and reflecting the outstanding range of his own singing voice) has been divided in this arrangement, phrase by phrase, between tenor and bass to enable the choir to give it the relentless drive that it demands.

52. Sing we and Chant it

A five-part madrigal might seem ambitious for a school choir. This one, from Thomas Morley's (c. 1557–1602) *First Book of Ballets to Five Voices* of 1595 is not over-demanding. The enjoyment of its light but rich texture will be reward enough for the effort required and will convey the heart-on-sleeve joy in artistic participation characteristic of the Elizabethans. This mood may reflect Morley's Roman Catholic background, in contrast to the Puritanical leanings which were gaining prevalence in Norwich, his home city.

53. Song for Mothering Day

The words for the male voices should either echo those of lines 1 and 3 of each verse (that is, twice each line of words); or reiterate "There grew in heav'n a Linden tree," as a refrain, the consonants being almost wholly subdued.

Index to titles and *first lines*